Gross National Product
of Czechoslovakia in Monetary
and Real Terms, 1946-58

STUDIES IN ECONOMICS

of the

ECONOMICS RESEARCH CENTER

of the

UNIVERSITY OF CHICAGO

Gross National Product of Czechoslovakia in Monetary and Real Terms, 1946-58

By

BORIS P. PESEK

THE UNIVERSITY OF CHICAGO PRESS

Chicago & London

Library of Congress Catalog Card Number: 65-14429

THE UNIVERSITY OF CHICAGO PRESS, CHICAGO & LONDON
The University of Toronto Press, Toronto 5, Canada

To Milena

Preface

THIS MONOGRAPH, stating in summary form the results of my work on the national product of Czechoslovakia, could not have been written without generous support from the Ford Foundation Area Research Fellowship (1954–56) and without a travel grant from the Social Science Research Council (1962).

During my work on the accounts covering the period 1946–53, Professors Earl J. Hamilton, Milton Friedman, and Bert Hoselitz let me draw freely on their funds of knowledge and experience. Professor Hamilton helped me improve substantially the finished manuscript.

My colleagues in the East European National Income Project of Columbia University discussed with me the innumerable issues that bedevil national-income accounting. Their detailed knowledge of economies of the Soviet type was a source not only of aid but of inspiration as well.

My wife helped me in innumerable ways while I was working on the manuscript in the United States and bore with me almost gracefully when I felt obliged to spend a substantial amount of time in the United Nations and Austrian libraries rather than in the castles, galleries, and cathedrals of France.

To all I am deeply grateful.

BORIS P. PESEK

MICHIGAN STATE UNIVERSITY
February 14, 1964

vii

Contents

I

Gross National Product in Current Monetary Units

II

Gross National Product in Real Terms

Tables

1

Introduction

IN THIS MONOGRAPH I present summaries of my estimates of
the gross national product of Czechoslovakia from 1946 to 1958.
This country is about the size of the state of Illinois, and has a
population of more than fourteen million. Czechoslovakia was
created after World War I out of several parts of the Austro-
Hungarian Empire: the Kingdom of Bohemia, belonging to the
Austrian part of the empire, was joined to Slovakia and Sub-
Ruthenia, belonging to the Hungarian part. Before World War
II, the nation was one of the few in Central and Eastern Europe
that enjoyed a genuine democracy. This was partly due, no doubt,
to the aspirations of the people and to the determined leadership
of Tomáš Garrigue Masaryk and Eduard Beneš. The fact that
Czechoslovakia completely lacked an aristocracy—this class hav-
ing been killed or exiled during the religious wars—probably
helped the nation to follow the democratic course.

Economically, the new state was far from homogeneous. It contained the highly industrialized Bohemia and Silesia; richly agricultural and partly industrial Moravia; very poor agricultural
Slovakia; and a medieval backwater of Europe, Sub-Ruthenia.
The last, however, was lost to the Soviet Union after the last
war. During the interwar period the development of the country
was mixed. Culturally, it was a period of an unprecedented
growth. The high level of education found in the Austrian part
of the country was rapidly extended to the Hungarian part. Literature, poetry, drama, opera, and music flourished. Economically,
the fates were less kind. The huge industrial complex of Bohemia
and Silesia had dimensions appropriate to the Austro-Hun-
garian Empire. When the economic curtain of national boundaries
descended in 1918 and separated these industries from a major
part of their markets, substantial difficulties were inevitable. The
new government, observing hyperinflations raging all around, was
determined to follow a responsible monetary and fiscal policy;
it therefore entrusted its management to a man who, with more

1

virtue than economic sense, attempted to restore the foreign-exchange value of the Czech crown to its prewar level. This strongly deflationary policy meant that Czechoslovakia did not find the Great Depression an altogether new experience.

During the Second World War, Czechoslovakia again became an industrial complex dimensioned to serve a much greater territory. Since the Czechs and Moravians were not obliged to serve in the armed forces, the labor pool available for the German war machine was one of the best in Europe. In addition, distances from the Anglo-American bomber bases and, one suspects, the reluctance of the Allies to bomb Czechoslovakia created a sort of sanctuary. After the war, the Czechoslovak government that arrived from London found itself in possession of an undamaged, even enriched, country. Moreover, the government found that it owned most of the country directly. For this, there were five major reasons.

First, the prewar depression had caused the government to subsidize a substantial number of banking and industrial enterprises by purchases of stocks. Second, very late in the thirties the government had engaged in two spectacular purchases. The Petchek family, which owned substantial parts of the industry and mining located in the western part of Bohemia, and the Rothschild family (the Vienna branch), which owned a sizable industrial complex in Silesia, offered to sell their holdings to the only purchaser with sufficient resources to buy—and pay with dollars—and with enough foresight to ignore the dismal short-run future of these properties. Third, during the war the Jewish population of Czechoslovakia was exterminated by the Germans, and their property was merged with other German properties in Czechoslovakia. After the war, the considerable holdings of those two hundred and fifty thousand people passed, along with other German property, into the hands of the government as war booty. Fourth, the large holdings of German and Austrian financial and industrial interests in Czechoslovakia, as well as the new plants built during the war, also became war booty. Fifth, all German-speaking former Czechoslovak citizens who after the Munich crisis accepted German citizenship were deported as enemy aliens, and their property was confiscated. More than two and one-half million people who very probably owned more than one-fifth of the wealth in Czechoslovakia were thus dispossessed by the government.

While no estimates are available, I believe that as a result of all these causes, the Czechoslovak government, at the end of 1946, owned outright at least one-half of all industrial enterprises, including all the major ones; one-half of banking; and more than thirty per cent of land, private housing, and non-industrial business properties. Rail transport and much of the road transport already belonged to the government, so productive facilities were to a great extent government-owned even before the government nationalized by decree all remaining private banking and industry in 1946 and before a law nationalized all remaining private businesses in 1948.

Thus at the end of World War II Czechoslovakia fully satisfied the requirements said to be necessary for a successful experiment in planning. Industry was well developed, but there were still reserves of agricultural population available for shifts into any new industries. Moreover, an extremely large part of all the productive facilities of the nation belonged to the government. Thus the bitterness that normally could be expected to follow governmental expropriation was avoided. The population itself—if we judge by the election results of 1946—was quite willing to embark upon a planning experiment. This was a very important asset for the planners who elsewhere in Central and Eastern Europe had to face undisguised hostility from the population. For all these reasons the performance of the Czechoslovak economy is very interesting to a student either of planning or of economic development. The performance of this economy and of the planners of it is measured by my national-income accounts.

NATIONAL-INCOME ACCOUNTS

In my work, I used a highly simplified version of the accounting framework developed by the United States Department of Commerce. From my accounts I eliminated all imputed items. This decision was based on the fact that imputations generally rest on very shaky foundations and that in Czechoslovakia even those items that pass through the market are difficult to measure. Imputation, in these conditions, leaves an excessive scope for purely arbitrary decisions, each of which may be of minor importance but which, in the aggregate, may seriously affect the results obtained.

To measure the changes in real output, I used—with minor exceptions—prices that were current in the period 1947–48. It is my belief that these prices, before the introduction of very heavy turnover taxes in 1949, reflect factor costs fairly closely. A major exception is rental expenditures, which even in 1947–48 had no relationship to factor costs because of rent controls existing since 1939.

DATA USED

Data available for the period 1946–58 are extremely heterogeneous both in quality and in quantity. Whenever possible, I gave preference to series that covered the longest possible part of the period over series that, even though more refined, covered only a part of the period and were only estimated in the official statistics for the remainder.

In 1957, the government published for the first time a Statistical Yearbook, containing a wealth of information that previously had not been available. In general, it seemed advisable to treat the official reconstruction of the past performance of the economy with extreme caution. From 1946 on, Czechoslovakia was in the grip of a permanent organizational revolution: enterprises were classified and reclassified; industrial branches were defined and redefined; items like wages, profits, labor force, and the like were defined in constantly changing ways. Already in 1953 the official organ of Czech planners wrote: "The fact is that we do not have today dependable data on the production of our industry during the past years and that we shall be forced to reconstruct very laboriously and by the use of a great number of estimates the development of production during the first Five Year Plan."[1] In 1963 the journal of the Czech statisticians published six pages of fine print on organizational and definitional changes that had basically affected data-gathering during the preceding eighteen years.[2] From casual remarks found in the literature one gathers that in

[1] *Politická Ekonomie,* 1 (1953), p. 34.

[2] *Statistický Obzor,* 4 (1963), p. 52.

many cases corrections for organizational and definitional changes were based simply on a crude estimate of a correction factor to be applied to an existing series.

For all these reasons it seemed that the best results could be achieved by using very simple accounts, relying on statistical evidence of a fairly basic type, and preferring contemporary figures to figures created years after the fact by the official statistician pressed to prepare continuous series for the Yearbook.

RESULTS

Before I present my results, the reader may wish to inquire into the reliability of my estimates. One way of doing so is to compare them with the accounts prepared for the years 1947, 1948, 1955, and 1956 by the Research Project on National Income in East Central Europe.[3] The Project took an approach fundamentally different from mine. It decided to concentrate on a few selected years and to prepare for these years accounts of exceptional detail and refinement. While I concentrated on major items likely to reflect general trends, the Project expended great effort in estimating even such minor items as wages of domestics. While I eliminated all imputed items, the Project estimated all major imputed items (imputed incomes of farmers and homeowners) and many minor items. Consequently, the two sets of accounts are not exactly comparable. The results obtained are shown in Table A.

Imputed incomes account for most of the differences between the results shown. Imputed consumption in the Project's accounts amounts, in the four years covered, to 23, 24, 7, and 7 billion crowns, respectively. Subtraction of these amounts brings the two estimates into close accord, with the exception of figures for the year 1948; that year, because of the coup d'état in February and the major nationalization of enterprises resulting from it, presents a confusing picture. According to the Project, however, money consumption adjusted for imputed items decreased from 1947 to 1956 by 50 per cent; my own estimate indicates a decrease of 47 per cent—a negligible difference for a period of nine years. Since the

[3] It is only fair to mention, however, that these two sets of accounts were not arrived at completely independently: I served as a consultant to the Project.

paths by which these two estimates were reached are fundamentally different, the similarity of results is striking. The government account also shows great similarities both in absolute size and in relative changes over time. Sizable differences in absolute terms appear in the case of the investment account, even though the absolute changes in these accounts (after correction for imputed amounts equal to +7, −5, −4, and −11 billion crowns) from 1946 to 1956 amount to 10 billion crowns in the Project's estimate and to 12 billion crowns in my estimates. With respect to the gross national product as a whole, my estimates assert a slightly smaller increase than the Project's estimates: the (money)

TABLE A

COMPARISON OF PRESENT RESULTS WITH RESULTS OBTAINED BY THE
RESEARCH PROJECT ON NATIONAL INCOME IN
EAST CENTRAL EUROPE, 1948, 1949, 1955, AND 1956

(In Billions of Current Crowns)

YEAR	GNP		CONSUMPTION		GOVERNMENT		INVESTMENT	
	Project	Pesek	Project	Pesek	Project	Pesek	Project	Pesek
1947[a]	246	220	179	152	47	50	20	17
1948[a]	286	275	186	182	50	54	49	39
1955[b]	151	128	83	76	31	29	37	24
1956[b]	162	139	86	81	28	29	48	29

[a] Source: Thad P. Alton, *Czechoslovak National Income and Product, 1947–48 and 1955–56*, pp. 11–21.
[b] Source: *ibid.*, p. 234.

figures drop by 37 per cent from 1947 to 1956, while the Project estimates this drop as only 35 per cent. Again, the difference, given the length of the period, is negligible.

In view of the basic differences in the method of constructing the two estimates, the similarity of results is highly encouraging and tends to reinforce my confidence in both sets of accounts. Consequently, I consider the two sets of accounts to be complementary rather than competitive. The Project's accounts provide richness of detail not matched in the series for any other country of the Soviet bloc. My own accounts, while much less finely structured, provide continuous coverage for a period of thirteen years and give estimates of the changes in the real magnitudes in addition to estimates expressed in nominal terms.

PRESENTATION OF RESULTS

My detailed discussion of methods and sources required almost three hundred pages, many of which contain items very expensive to print: statistical tables and numerous references to foreign-language publications. Consequently, I have decided to present to the general reader only the key tables and my discussion of some of the key decisions made. Everything else is relegated to a mimeographed appendix that is available on request from Boris P. Pesek, Department of Economics, Michigan State University, East Lansing, Michigan.

PART I

*Gross National Product in Current
Monetary Units*

2

Personal Income

Estimating personal income and its disposition presents much greater difficulties than estimating other components of the gross national income. The main source of these difficulties is that, while most of the other elements of the gross national product are under complete control of the government and subject to its budgeting procedures, many of the components of the personal-income accounts have either not been measured directly by the government, or have not been reported in the available statistical sources.

Complete and dependable official data exist on transfer payments, which in the case of Czechoslovakia amount to approximately 15 per cent of personal income. Wage and salary payments for the years 1953 and following are also available from official series. For the period 1946–52 somewhat different techniques have to be used. The remaining components of personal income rest on less firm foundations. Fortunately, their weight in the total personal income is small.

LABOR-FORCE ESTIMATES

Data on average wages and average salaries were used to compute wage and salary bills during the period 1946–52. To utilize these and to provide a factual basis for handling some of the less important and more troublesome segments of the personal-income table, I found it necessary to prepare a statistical series on the distribution of the income-receiving population among different occupations (Table 1).

Official labor-force data are available for the year 1948 and the period 1950–58. The official tables are so constructed, however, that they do not suit the purposes of my own estimates, namely, the presentation of data on average incomes of various occupational groups. Still, the official total at least of the non-farming force can be used for the evaluation of my own estimates, which are pieced together from a substantial number of separate

11

sources. It is noteworthy that the average discrepancy between my own estimates and the official data amounts to only fifty thousand persons: this could lead to an error of 1.4 per cent in my income estimates. While my estimates, however, in three cases out of four show a labor force bigger than the one shown officially, the official estimates exclude apprentices, who in 1948 numbered 151 thousand and in 1952, 125 thousand.[1] If each apprentice had an income amounting to one-third of the average income, any error

TABLE 1

OCCUPATIONAL STRUCTURE OF THE LABOR FORCE, 1946–52 [1]

(In Thousands of Persons)

Occupation	1946	1947	1948	1949	1950	1951	1952
Self-employed:							
Farmers..................	582	687	687	662	587	662	543
Entrepreneurs.............	369	369	257	205	153	114	91
Professionals..............	23	23	23	.....	.....	.....	.....
Employed:							
Salaried employees..........	589	605	646	704	823	758	816
Agricultural workers........	509	404	404	378	329	364	260
Members of farm collectives...	.....	.....	.....	25	75	40	144
Salaried workers............	586	591	2,241	2,347	2,458	2,575	2,697
Wage workers..............	1,554	1,564					
Others....................	138	153	167	182	196	211	225
Total farm.................	1,091	1,091	1,091	1,065	1,026	1,026	947
Total non-farm..............	3,258	3,305	3,352	3,439	3,595	3,656	3,822
Grand total..............	4,349	4,396	4,443	4,504	4,621	4,682	4,769
Official total farm............	.....	.....	2,244	.....	2,063	1,927	1,855
Official total non-farm.........	.....	.....	3,301	.....	3,514	3,664	3,745
Official grand total..........	.....	.....	5,545	.....	5,577	5,591	5,600

in my national income estimates caused by an overestimate of the labor force would disappear. Any deviation in the incomes of apprentices from this amount would cause an error in my income estimates; but this error must be substantially smaller than 1 per cent of the total income of the non-farming population.

The discrepancy between the official estimates of the farm population and my own is huge. The difference is of no consequence, however, because the estimate of farm population is not used in my estimates of national income: it is included in Table 1 only to provide an internal check on the consistency of the annual

[1] Statistická Ročenka, 1959, p. 101.

estimates. It might be mentioned in passing that the main reason for the difference between my own and the official estimates of the farm labor force is definitional. The official estimates classify as farm worker everyone living on a farm who is older than 14. My definition is much more restrictive.

WAGE AND SALARY BILLS

The calculation of wages and salaries is based on two distinct sets of data. For the period 1946–52 I have used data on average wages and average salaries (Table 2) and data on the number of workers and employees (Table 1) to obtain the total wage and

TABLE 2

AVERAGE MONTHLY WAGES AND SALARIES, 1946–52
(In Crowns)

Year	Wages	Salaries
1946.	532.6	869.0
1947.	643.6	1,007.6
1948.	722.2	1,075.6
1949.	765.8	1,131.6
1950.	908.6	1,251.8
1951.	1,004.4	1,295.2
1952.	1,241.2	1,485.8

salary bill. For the period 1953–58 I used official figures that show the total wage and salary bill in the socialistic sector of the economy. While these series cover the period 1948–52 as well, I did not consider it advisable to use them instead of my own estimates: the number of employees in the non-socialistic sector of the economy was falling rapidly during this period and so the official data contain an upward bias.

In the years 1953 and following, the official series was used to good advantage. It should be pointed out that wages and salaries for the years 1953–56 were taken from the Yearbook for 1957; the following Yearbooks present another series that is based on a definition used by official statisticians for the year 1957 and following. In these more recent Yearbooks the data for the period 1948–56 have been recalculated. The root of this discrepancy is to be found in the treatment of the first six weeks of sickness of salaried employees. Until 1956 this cost was borne by enterprises; since 1957 the cost has been borne by the National Insurance Company. Acceptance of this *ex post facto* adjustment of wage and salary bill would have required adjustment of transfer payments, receipts of the National Insurance Company, and tax receipts of the state. Since data for such an adjustment are missing, and since even the official recalculation does not rely on a genuine recalculation, but on the application of an estimated ratio of the salary bill based on the old and the new definitions, I have decided to use in my tables the current definition of wages and salaries.

Incomes of employees in the private sector have been estimated

TABLE 3

INCOME OF PRIVATE EMPLOYEES, 1953–58

Year	Number of Private Employees	Average Wage of Industrial Workers (Crowns)	Total Private Wages (Million Crowns)
1953..........	7,000	13,716	96.0
1954..........	9,000	14,810	132.3
1955..........	7,000	15,096	105.7
1956..........	7,000	15,492	108.4
1957..........	5,000	15,576	77.9
1958..........	2,000	15,900	31.8

on the basis of the number of employees in the private sector and on the assumption that their monthly wage was the same as in the socialistic sector (Table 3). While this is likely to overestimate their incomes, the sums involved are small.

TRANSFER PAYMENTS

The next substantial item in the personal-income accounts is transfer payments. Official data dealing with this item are more than adequate. They are presented in Table 4.

REMAINING ITEMS IN THE PERSONAL-INCOME ACCOUNT

After the wage bill, the salary bill, and transfer payments have been dealt with, the greater part of the personal-income account is complete. Of the relatively minor components left, only two remained significant during the entire period. One was the income of farmers, the other the income of farm workers and of members of agricultural collectives. Other elements significant at the beginning of the period became extremely minor by the end (incomes of entrepreneurs) or were eliminated completely (incomes of professionals). Finally, it is necessary to account for rental income and interest income. Most of the minor components proved to be major problems from the standpoint of preparing of satisfactory income estimates.

TABLE 4

TRANSFER PAYMENTS, 1946–58
(In Millions of Crowns)

Year	Cash Sickness Benefits	Old-Age Benefits	Supple-mentary Social Care	Total
1946........	884	1,209	....	2,093
1947........	1,248	1,427	....	2,675
1948........	1,461	1,983	....	3,444
1949........	1,881	4,728	....	6,609
1950........	2,428	5,262	....	7,690
1951........	2,981	5,449	....	8,430
1952........	3,140	5,523	....	8,663
1953........	3,747	6,080	....	9,827
1954........	4,648	6,618	62	11,328
1955........	4,891	6,894	64	11,849
1956........	5,137	7,386	110	12,633
1957........	6,730	8,909	259	15,898
1958........	6,142	9,680	268	16,090

RENTS

In 1946 this part of personal income amounted to only 702 million crowns. This amount was kept unchanged until 1952. In 1952 a new law was passed imposing a series of very high taxes on incomes derived from rents. All rent receipts became subject to a flat tax of 45 per cent. An additional 30 per cent was given to the local authorities for maintenance and repair. Only the remaining 25 per cent could be paid to the landlords. Budget studies covering the most recent period (1958) indicate that the non-farm population spends approximately 2 per cent of its income for rent. In 1958 this would amount to 1,538 million crowns. Out of this amount, 778 million crowns are rents of those living in houses belonging to the state and local governments. This leaves 760 million crowns for the private house-owners, an amount only slightly higher than the one shown for the year 1946. After subtracting 342 million crowns (45 per cent) paid to the state in taxes and 228 million crowns received by local governments for repair and maintenance, 190 million crowns are left to the private house-owner. It might be noted that the yield of the state house tax in 1958 amounted to 404 million crowns. Because owner-occupied housing is taxed, but at a low rate, direct comparison is impossible. This sum (only slightly higher than my estimate of the tax received from house-owners renting to others) indicates that I may be overestimating the net privately received rent, but the sum is negligible. Additional adjustment would be arbitrary and would not affect the personal-income estimate perceptibly. Thus the estimate above was kept and extended to cover the years 1953–57.

INTEREST

The National Bank of Czechoslovakia and the State Statistical Office published detailed reports on the amount of deposits from 1946 to 1949; after that date the time series stops and is resumed only in 1954. For calculating the amount of interest received, I assumed that the total amount of time deposits from 1949 to 1952 did not increase at all. This seems hardly credible: during a period in which personal income almost doubled, savings would certainly be expected to increase. But there is evidence that my assumption is close to reality. First, the time-deposit accounts, while increasing during the entire period for which data are available, do so at a sharply decreasing rate. The shift in new savings from amounts reaching billions of crowns in 1946–47 to amounts calculated in millions in 1950 is explained by three factors: a low rate of interest and a high rate of inflation, increases in social-security care, and lack of investment opportunities.

I calculated the amount of interest received on the basis of data for time deposits during the period 1946 through 1949; the amount calculated for the year 1949 I then kept constant for the next four years. The calculation of interest payments was based on the official interest rate as published by the National Bank of Czechoslovakia.

UNCLASSIFIED EMPLOYMENTS

The tabulation of the special tax returns for 1946 included the category "unclassified employments." The average income in this category is far below the minimum that would support a person (103 crowns a month) and individuals in this category had very few dependents. (Returns submitted by 138,150 heads of families covered 168,333 persons.) I was unable to find any definite statement as to what people were included in this category. My guess is that the group included mostly soldiers, with some minor segments of the population, such as part-time students, thrown in. As the income of soldiers during this period was not increased enough to invite self-congratulatory comments by government officials, I made the most generous assumption I could: the incomes of soldiers increased percentagewise as much as wages did during the same period. As the sum concerned is extremely slight, my generosity or niggardliness could not perceptibly change the final personal-income accounts.

PROFESSIONS

The group called "professions" contains persons engaged in more or less independent intellectual pursuits: lawyers, physicians, writers, musicians, composers, artists, and the like. In 1949 all lawyers became employees of the Department of Justice and all physicians, employees of the National Health Service. Recurrent newspaper reports indicate, however, that a number of doctors still make themselves available for private consultations and apparently attempts are made to regulate this practice. Many performing artists, painters, and sculptors receive income that is not reported in the column of wages and salaries (as are royalties).

For the year 1946 data on the incomes of professionals are available thanks to the special tax report. For the following two years I made the assumption that their incomes rose by the same percentage as salaries. From 1949 on, no information on these professional incomes is available. A small arbitrary sum was assigned to this category of incomes and increased proportionally somewhat more than total personal income.

ENTREPRENEURS, CRAFTSMEN, AND RETAILERS

The entrepreneurial group, which before 1948 constituted an economically important segment of the total labor force, was whittled away in subsequent years in a great many ways. Two such ways were the nationalization of all enterprises employing more than fifty persons and the high taxes imposed upon those who employed hired labor. In 1953 some thirty-three thousand people were still engaged in handicraft, and a like number were engaged in some combination of handicraft and retail business. This group achieved its greatest prosperity in 1947, when its

TABLE 5

ENTREPRENEURIAL INCOME, 1946–58

Year	Number of Persons (Thousands)	Income (Million Crowns)
1946..........	369	3,062
1947..........	369	3,683
1948..........	257	3,079
1949..........	205	2,433
1950..........	153	2,151
1951..........	114	1,004
1952..........	91	1,065
1953..........	80	937
1954..........	70	835
1955..........	60	731
1956..........	50	624
1957..........	45	479
1958..........	23	308

income rose by 20 per cent over the previous year. There are no data for the incomes of these people in subsequent years. In this case, the difficulties of estimating the incomes received by this group were so great that I was unable to reach a satisfactory solution. It is my belief that the incomes of those who succeeded in keeping their businesses rose considerably, despite the efforts of the regime to tax away their earnings. Most of these people provided personal services of some kind or other, and such occupations are extremely unsuitable for efficient price-fixing and efficient tax-collecting, especially in times of imperfectly suppressed inflation. I therefore made the assumption that the incomes of this group rose as fast as the incomes of the fastest-moving group in Czechoslovakia, the workers (Table 5). My guess would be that even this is not a great enough rate of change.

According to a single figure available for the year 1951, the income of landlords and of people engaged in handicraft and retail trade was 1.3 billion crowns. My own estimate for the same year is somewhat higher: 1.8 billion crowns. Since personal disposable income during this year was 60 billion crowns, the difference is not significant; I kept my estimate because the official data in all probability suffer from under-reporting.

FARMERS AND MEMBERS OF COLLECTIVE FARMS

There were no data that would permit me to approach the problem of farm incomes as directly as the incomes of wage and salary workers. At the same time, farm incomes are still substantial enough to require great care.

TABLE 6

ESTIMATE OF FARM INCOME, 1947–58

Year	Income (Million Crowns)	Value of Sales (Million Crowns)	Output of Marketed Com-modities (Index)	Consumer Prices of Agricul-tural Com-modities (Index)	Prices of Marketed Agricul-tural Com-modities (Index)	Esti-mated Income (Million Crowns)	Known Income of Col-lectives (Million Crowns)	Esti-mated Private Farm Income (Million Crowns)
1946...	2,950	6,469						
1947...		6,074				2,766		2,760
1948...		6,742				3,070		3,070
1949...		8,023	79.2	103.72		3,653	n.a.	n.a.
1950...			98.5	162.14		5,710	n.a.	n.a.
1951...			98.2	185.37		6,529	n.a.	n.a.
1952...			99.7	200.33	810	7,055	n.a.	n.a.
1953...			105.5		898	8,278	1,714	6,564
1954...			97.5		1,056	8,996	2,146	6,850
1955...			105.3		1,207	11,105	2,704	8,399
1956...			110.7		1,282	12,399	3,388	9,011
1957...			114.8		1,306	13,099	5,752	7,347
1958...			123.3		1,321	14,231	6,728	7,503

For the first year under study, the income of the farming population is known, thanks again to the special tax report. For the next four years there are good data pertaining to the value of sales made by the agricultural sector. I assumed that the ratio of the value of inputs and outputs remained unchanged, and on this basis I estimated the income of the agricultural sector. Then comes a hiatus: for the years 1950–52, no really good data are available. The only acceptable technique here was to combine the index of the prices of farm commodities at the retail level and the index of marketed output of farm sector into an index of the changes of farmers' income (Table 6). This is almost certain to overestimate the income for this sector because during this time there was a substantial shift of the population away from the farms. The manpower losses occasioned by this shift were offset by the use of machinery and fertilizers. This upward bias is counteracted (and I hope approximately balanced) by the increasing farm subsidies granted newly established farm collectives. Nevertheless, this series is one of the more doubtful ones.

FARM WORKERS

The considerable decrease in the number of farm workers during the period is due to three main factors: first, land reform made it possible for farm workers to acquire land; second, employment opportunities existed in other branches of the economy where much higher wages were being paid; and third, it was possible for workers to enter collective farms.

Wages paid to farm workers were subject to government regulation of wage and salary scales. An official source stated that policy of the wage authorities was to keep changes in the wages of farm workers on a par with changes in wages paid to industrial workers. The account dealing with wages of farm workers was therefore prepared on this basis. After 1952, farm workers on state farms were included in the wage report on the socialistic sector of the economy; privately employed farm workers were non-existent.

SUMMARY

Using the data and techniques described above, I calculated the personal income of the citizens of Czechoslovakia. It will be noticed that no imputed incomes were included. The difficulty of calculating this portion of income, even for countries with many statistical data available, is staggering. Even then only part of the imputed income is calculated. Any attempt to carry out such computation for Czechoslovakia seems inadvisable at present. From total personal income I deducted social-security payments and personal tax and non-tax payments to arrive at the final figure for personal disposable income. Before the personal-income table is finally presented, it will be necessary to discuss in the next chapter consumption expenditures for good and services, with which disposable personal income must be compared.

3

Personal Consumption Expenditures

Dᴀᴛᴀ ꜰᴏʀ ᴘᴇʀꜱᴏɴᴀʟ ᴄᴏɴꜱᴜᴍᴘᴛɪᴏɴ expenditures during the years 1946–52 are available except for the year 1951. Exponential trend gave an excellent fit and was used to interpolate the missing year. For the following period, detailed data showing retail sales are available. Several adjustments had to be made, however, to convert them to personal consumption expenditures. Except for one instance, all these adjustments rely on excellent statistical

TABLE 7

RETAIL SALES AND PERSONAL CONSUMPTION EXPENDITURES, 1953–58
(In Millions of Crowns)

Type of Expenditure	1953	1954	1955	1956	1957	1958
Total retail sales..............	65,985	72,975	78,283	83,520	89,247	90,233
Plus: Rent receipts of hotels...	392	320	327	367	348	371
Retail sales of wholesalers	300	440	596	600	600	600
Farm market sales.......	2,030	1,168	1,252	1,336	1,071	1,353
Receipts of communal enterprises............	1,200	1,215	1,387	1,176	1,430	1,511
Rent receipts..........	1,093	1,209	1,263	1,346	1,393	1,538
Transportation expenditures................	527	673	829	900	1,098	1,192
Less: Purchases of building materials..............	1,588	1,593	1,672	1,670	1,675	1,192
Purchases of farm inputs.	1,452	1,331	1,677	1,951	1,967	2,255
Purchases of business enterprises............	4,443	4,410	4,652	4,310	4,759	5,529
Equals: Total consumption expenditures..............	64,318	70,968	75,902	81,275	86,601	86,523

evidence. From retail sales it was necessary to subtract sales of building materials used for private housing construction, farm inputs (fertilizers, implements, etc.), and retail sales to business enterprises. It was necessary to add rents, receipts of hotels, retail sales of wholesalers, farm-market sales, sales of communal enterprises to households (local transportation, dry-cleaning, hairdressing, repair work, etc.), rent payments, and long-distance transportation expenditures. Data are available for each of these adjustments except retail sales to business enterprises. But the statistical material does show the cost structure in the two major

22

TABLE 8

PERSONAL INCOME AND DISPOSITION OF INCOME, 1946-58

(In Millions of Crowns)

Type of Income	1946	1947	1948	1949	1950	1951	1952	1953	1954	1955	1956	1957	1958
Personal income	29,379	34,496	38,949	46,470	57,505	62,596	68,203	73,379	81,197	86,412	93,983	98,883	102,215
Self-employed	6,288	6,752	6,472	7,137	7,916	7,593	8,815	9,285	9,906	11,914	13,107	13,768	14,634
Farmers	2,950	2,766	3,070	3,653	5,710	6,529	7,055	6,564	6,850	8,399	9,011	7,347	7,503
Members of farm collectives								1,714	2,146	2,704	3,388	5,752	6,728
Entrepreneurs	3,069	3,683	3,079	2,433	2,151	1,004	1,065	937	835	731	624	479	308
Professions	269	303	323	50	55	60	65	70	75	80	85	90	95
Employed	21,324	25,468	29,468	32,879	41,053	45,727	51,021	53,933	59,708	62,375	66,552	68,891	71,142
Salary employees	6,146	7,318	8,332	9,564	12,370	12,411	14,556						
Wage workers	13,672	16,645	19,424	21,571	26,805	31,033	34,556						
Agricultural workers	1,338	1,283	1,439	1,430	1,474	1,803	1,365						
Others	168	222	273	314	404	480	544	674	727	742	761	766	771
Employees of socialistic enterprises								53,163	58,849	61,527	65,683	68,047	70,339
Employees of private enterprises									132	106	108	78	32
Other income	734	791	825	846	846	846	334	334	255	274	297	326	349
Interest	32	89	123	144	144	144	144	144	65	84	107	136	159
Rent	702	702	702	702	702	702	190	190	190	190	190	190	190
Transfer payments	2,093	2,675	3,444	6,609	7,690	8,430	8,663	9,827	11,328	11,849	12,633	15,898	16,090
Cash sickness compensation	884	1,248	1,461	1,881	2,428	2,981	3,140	3,747	4,648	4,891	5,137	6,730	6,142
Old-age benefits	1,209	1,427	1,983	4,728	5,262	5,449	5,523	6,080	6,618	6,894	7,386	8,909	9,680
Other									62	64	110	259	268
Less: Personal contributions for social security	1,060	1,190	1,260										
Less: Personal tax and non-tax payments	1,960	2,321	2,625	3,019	4,620	1,860	4,020	7,639	8,644	9,116	9,728	9,950	10,110
Equals: Personal disposable income	27,419	32,175	36,324	43,451	52,885	60,736	64,183	65,740	72,553	77,296	84,255	88,933	92,105
Less: Personal consumption expenditures	25,577	30,472	36,513	43,992	54,286	61,365	70,240	64,318	70,968	75,902	81,276	86,610	86,523
Equals: Personal savings	1,842	1,703	− 189	− 541	− 1,401	− 629	− 6,057	1,422	1,585	1,394	2,980	2,332	5,582

branches of the productive sector, industry and construction. These accounts, after reporting the amounts of purchases of raw materials, semifinished goods and materials from other production enterprises, and expenditures for power supplies and wages, contain an item called "miscellaneous small purchases." These are purchases of supplies from sources other than "productive enterprises": only retail enterprises may be thus classified. The results are shown in Table 7.

In the preceding two sections I have presented the description of my estimates of personal income and consumption. Now these two estimates are combined and presented in Table 8, showing personal income and disposition of income.

CONCLUSION

The personal income tables consist of two independently measured magnitudes: personal income and personal consumption expenditures. Each of these magnitudes was subjected to all the tests available, and both appeared to stand these tests very well. When studying the link connecting these two series, namely, personal savings, I found that their behavior could well be explained by available independent evidence. On all these grounds, I believe that personal income and disposition of income estimates are a reliable reflection of reality and may be used with a considerable degree of confidence.

4

Other Components of Gross National Income and Product

I SHALL NOW turn to the estimates of the other components of the gross national product.

GOVERNMENT ACCOUNTS

In most countries the budgetary procedures are such that published data are not suitable for use in the national-income accounts before they are extensively rearranged and classified in certain broad categories required by national-income accounting. In the case of Czechoslovakia, care must also be exercised to avoid special pitfalls. First, in contrast to the usual financial practices of various states, in Czechoslovakia there was very little connection in the years 1949–53 between the appropriation acts as presented to and approved by the parliament and actual cash expenditures by the state administration. In the period 1946–53 the average discrepancy between the sums appropriated and spent amounted to more than 20 per cent, with 8 per cent as the minimum and 31 per cent as the maximum. Another difficulty is that the Czechoslovak budgeting procedure underwent major changes during this period. Those changes, if neglected, make comparison of the data for different years impossible.

The major revisions consist of the integration of state expenditures based on bonded debt in the period 1946–58, and the adjustment required by the greatly enlarged scope of the budget in 1953. Until 1953 the state collected substantial funds from enterprises and made them available to other enterprises for investment purposes. Such funds were called "state investments." Subsequently this practice was dropped, and the only investments reported separately are investments in purely governmental objects: schools, administrative buildings, etc. It will be noticed that the column containing only the government expenditures proper, excluding investments, reveals a substantial degree of

25

continuity lacking in other columns precisely because of this dual treatment of investments in the period 1946–53 and following.

TRANSFER PAYMENTS

The next adjustment required for the whole period under study concerned transfer payments. On the credit side of the government account it was necessary to eliminate all transfer payments. On the debit side it was necessary to eliminate state expenditures on transfer payments and the state-covered deficit of the institutions paying all the other transfer payments. In summary, the adjustment necessary is shown below:

Credit	*Debit*
Total government receipts	Total government expenditures
Less:	*Less:*
Receipts to cover transfer payments made by the state (equal to transfer payments)	Transfer payments made by the state
Less:	*Less:*
Transfer payments made by the National Insurance Co.	Deficit of the National Insurance Co.
Plus:	
Receipts of the National Insurance Co.	
Equals:	*Equals:*
Net receipts of the government	Government purchases of goods and services

This shows all the adjustments that were made in the data for state receipts and expenditures. The state receipts are presented in Table 9 and the state expenditures in Table 10.

GROSS DOMESTIC INVESTMENT

Closely connected with the state budget was the gross domestic investment. A substantial portion of this investment was financed directly by the state; only a minor portion was financed from funds which, until 1952, were provided by the enterprises themselves. The division of expenditures was not considered important, and indeed it is not. After 1952 a new statistical series appearing in the Statistical Yearbook eliminated entirely the distinction between the state-financed and enterprise-financed investments: they are all reported as investments of the state.

As in the case of most Czech statistical series, the data for the year 1953 are of dubious value. The monetary reform broke up the year into two parts, and the accounting changes connected with the reform burdened the state and enterprise accountants to such a degree that even the most basic data are lacking. The most nearly comparable series on investments in money terms is shown by column 5 in Table 11 from 1949 to 1952; by column

TABLE 9

REVENUE OF THE GOVERNMENT, 1946–58
(In Millions of Crowns)

	1	2	3	4	5	6	7	8	9	10
Year	Appropriations	Comparability Adjustment	Total Comparable Appropriations	Receipts	Receipts on Accounts of Social Security Fund	Total Receipts	Transfer Payments	Net Receipts	Comparability Adjustment Due to FNE[a]	Total Receipts
1946...	7,558	......	7,558	8,403	2,120	10,523	2,093	8,430	....	8,430
1947...	9,680	......	9,680	2,360	2,360	11,814	2,674	9,139	....	9,139
1948...	11,379	......	11,379	13,996	2,520	16,516	3,444	13,072	....	13,072
1949...	17,864	......	17,864	22,721	5,443	28,163	6,609	21,554	....	21,554
1950...	26,386	......	26,386	29,609	6,764	36,373	7,890	28,483	....	28,483
1951...	33,304	......	33,304	43,772	4,086	51,858	8,430	48,928	....	48,928
1952...	64,857	13,400	51,457	71,671	9,407	81,087	8,663	72,415	13,400	59,015
1953...	87,041	30,754	56,288	93,041	......	93,041[b]	9,827	83,214	{14,794 520[b]	67,901
1954...	87,800	......	......	84,241	......	84,241	11,328	72,913	39,110	33,803
1955...	86,209	......	......	86,382	......	86,382	11,849	74,533	37,924	36,609
1956...	90,304	......	......	90,304	......	90,304	12,633	77,671	42,338	35,333
1957...	98,240	......	......	98,240	......	98,240	15,898	82,342	45,996	36,346
1958...	94,725	......	......	94,725	......	94,725	16,090	78,635	36,857	41,778

[a] FNE = Fund of the Nationalized Economy.
[b] Additional adjustment for the inclusion of budgetary organizations.

6 for 1953, and by column 10 from 1954 on. The reason is that before the monetary reform of 1953, rising costs during the year forced the investor to spend substantially more for investments than planned (col. 2). In 1953, prices ceased rising so drastically, and so the most dependable figures became those showing actual expenditures in money terms. Figures on planned expenditures in money terms then ceased to be available because planned investments were reported only in terms of expenditures expressed

TABLE 10

EXPENDITURES OF THE GOVERNMENT, 1946–58

(In Millions of Crowns)

Year	Appropriations (1)	Expenditures Based on Funded Debt (2)	Comparability Adjustment, Col. 6 Less Col. 7 (3)	Total Comparable Appropriations (4)	Expenditures (5)	Adjustment Due to FNE[a] (6)	Adjustment Due to NIC[b] (7)	Comparable Expenditures (8)	Deficit or Surplus of NIC (9)	Government Purchases of Investments, Goods and Services (10)	Government Purchases of Investments (11)	Government Purchases of Emergency Stocks of Consumer Goods (12)	Total Government Purchases of Other Goods and Services (13)
1946	12,800.0	1,900.0		14,700.0	11,695.0			11,695.0	− 27.0	11,722.0	2,250.0		9,472.0
1947	15,261.0	1,181.0		16,442.0	12,095.0			12,095.0	− 315.0	11,780.0	1,702.2		10,077.8
1948	13,411.2	1,935.2		15,346.4	15,917.4			15,917.4	924.4	14,993.4	4,049.4		10,944.0
1949	17,855.6			17,655.6	22,720.6			22,720.6	−1,166.4	21,554.2	11,928.2		9,626.0
1950	26,311.2			26,311.2	29,609.0			29,609.0	−1,125.8	28,483.2	15,787.0		12,696.2
1951	33,249.2			33,249.2	43,771.8			43,771.8	344.2	43,427.6	24,903.2	320.0	18,524.4
1952	64,716.4		13,200	51,505.6	71,671.0			55,649.2	+ 744.0	59,215.0	31,566.0	3,639.2	27,649.0
1953	86,182.0		20,533	55,649.2	86,182.0	14,572.8	15,960.0	55,649.2		55,649.2	33,400.0		22,249.2
1954	81,200.0		50,438	30,762.0	81,200.0	39,110.0	11,328.0	30,762.0		30,762.0	5,140.0		25,622.0
1955	86,039.0		49,773	36,266.0	83,900.0	37,924.0	11,849.0	34,127.0		34,127.0	5,452.0		28,675.0
1956	89,887.0		45,975	43,916.0	89,887.0	42,338.0	12,633.0	34,916.0		34,916.0	5,800.0		29,161.0
1957	97,919.0		61,894	36,125.0	97,919.0	45,996.0	15,898.0	36,025.0		36,025.0	7,059.0		28,966.0
1958	94,531.0		52,957	41,584.0	94,531.0	36,857.0	16,090.0	41,584.0		41,584.0	8,460.0		33,124.0

[a] FNE = Fund of the Nationalized Economy.

[b] NIC = National Insurance Company.

in constant crowns. Some additional adjustments, which had been unnecessary in the preceding period, had to be made, however. Local governments initiated "Actions Z and T"; these consisted of street and park improvements, local works requiring negligible amounts of materials and substantial amounts of labor. The value of these investments as reported in the Statistical Yearbook is the imputed value, based on reports made to the central government about the turnout of the local population. I have eliminated this item in my accounts along with all other imputed items.

TABLE 11

COMPONENTS OF GROSS DOMESTIC INVESTMENT, 1946–58

(In Millions of Crowns)

	1	2	3	4	5	6	7	8	9	10
Year	Appropriations Out of the State Budget: Original	Additional	Total Spent by the State	Investment Outside of the State Budget	Total Planned	Total Spent	Less: Actions Z and T	Less: Private Housing	Plus: Materials for Private Housing	Total Adjusted Investments
1946.....	5,015	......	2,250	1,000ᵃ	......	3,250	......	......	......	3,250
1947.....	......	......	1,402	3,247	......	4,948	......	......	......	4,984
1948.....	2,704	1,158	3,863	4,884	......	8,746	......	......	......	8,746
1949.....	4,920	7,008	11,928	5,880	10,800	17,808	......	......	......	17,808
1950.....	9,640	6,147	15,687	8,760	18,400	24,547	......	......	......	24,547
1951.....	15,440	9,463	24,903	4,560	20,000	29,463	......	......	......	29,463
1952.....	18,400	6,966	25,366	6,200	24,600	31,466	......	......	......	31,566
1953.....	......	......	......	......	......	33,400ᵃ	......	......	......	33,400
1954.....	......	......	......	......	......	20,000	377	1,090	580	19,113
1955.....	......	......	......	......	......	24,320	664	1,549	850	22,975
1956.....	......	......	......	......	......	29,771	855	3,233	1,681	27,364
1957.....	......	......	......	......	......	32,792	1,078	3,319	1,620	30,015
1958.....	......	......	......	......	......	31,983	888	1,552	879	30,322

ᵃ Rough estimate.

EMERGENCY STOCKS OF CONSUMER GOODS

There was another type of investment financed out of the conventional state budget: the accumulation of inventories of consumer goods. This buildup of inventories occurred in 1951 and 1952. Some maintain that these stocks were created to provide reserves for war; the fact that the stockpiling started just after the outbreak of the Korean war lends some support to this interpretation. The regime maintained silence for a long time about the purpose of the reserves. Then, after the monetary reform of 1953, a short note appeared in the house organ of the Czechoslovak planners:

> The reserves of consumer goods which have been built up by the state in the last two years assured by their size and composition not only [the success of] the reform of the market of June 1, 1953; they, along with the [production] possibilities of our industry, made it possible to march toward the systematic decreases of retail prices.

A similar statement, though much less specific, was made by Madame Jankovcová, Secretary of Supplies, in 1955.

Whatever the original purpose of these stocks, there is no doubt that they facilitated the monetary reform of 1953. As a separate and distinct part of the expenditures of the administration, these inventories must be expressed in the national-income accounts. As in several cases discussed previously, the necessary figures could only be estimated because the regime released absolutely no data about the magnitudes involved.

The same article quoted above, however, contains an estimate claiming that the value of goods thus released amounted to 4,500 million crowns. Lacking any more precise figures, I have decided to use this estimate. It should be emphasized, however, that it is entirely conceivable that not all the reserves were released in 1953. Madame Jankovcová's statement, in fact, strongly indicates that they were not.

NET FOREIGN INVESTMENT

Net foreign investment represents a comparatively minor part of the gross national product. For the entire period 1946–53, data on net foreign investment are available. For the following period, only data concerning the visible trade are available.

OTHER COMPONENTS

Since it proved impossible to gather any data showing the amount of business savings, this component of the national product accounts was consolidated with the statistical discrepancy into a single number for each year. I made no attempt to quantify the capital consumption allowance. Any estimate of this allow-

TABLE 12

DISPOSITION AND SOURCES OF GROSS NATIONAL PRODUCT, 1946–58
(In Millions of Crowns)

Type of Disbursement	1946	1947	1948	1949	1950	1951	1952	1953	1954	1955	1956	1957	1958
Consumer purchases	25,777	30,472	36,513	43,982	54,286	61,365	70,239	64,318	70,968	75,902	81,275	86,601	86,523
Gross savings:													
Gross personal savings	1,842	1,703	− 189	− 541	− 1,401	− 629	− 6,057	1,422	1,585	1,394	2,980	2,332	5,582
Gross enterprise savings[a]	730	2,746	5,947	6,603	11,047	− 1,214	9,013	− 16,986	9,869	14,535	19,663	20,094	17,209
Statistical discrepancy													
Taxes (including social-security benefits minus transfer payments)	8,430	9,139	13,072	21,554	28,483	48,928	59,015	67,901	33,803	36,609	35,333	36,346	41,778
Disposition of gross national expenditures	36,779	44,060	55,343	71,598	92,415	108,450	132,210	116,655	116,225	128,440	139,251	145,373	151,092
Consumer purchases	25,777	30,472	36,513	43,982	54,286	61,365	70,239	64,318	70,968	75,902	81,275	86,601	86,523
Gross domestic investment	3,250	4,950	8,746	17,808	24,547	29,463	31,566	33,400	19,113	22,975	27,364	30,015	30,322
Investment by persons	1,000	3,248	4,697	5,880	8,760	4,560	0	0	580	850	1,681	1,620	879
Investment by enterprises									13,393	16,673	19,883	21,336	20,983
Investment by government	2,250	1,702	4,049	11,928	15,787	24,903	31,566	33,400	5,140	5,452	5,800	7,059	8,460
Government investment (+) or disinvestment (−) in emergency stocks of consumer goods	0	0	0	0	0	+ 328	+ 3,940	− 4,500	0	0	0	0	0
Net foreign investment	− 1,720	− 1,440	− 860	182	886	− 1,230	30	1,188	522	888	1,451	− 209	1,123
Government purchases of noncapital goods and services	9,472	10,078	10,944	9,626	12,696	18,524	27,649	22,249	25,622	28,675	29,161	28,966	33,124
Sources of gross national product	36,779	44,060	55,343	71,598	92,415	108,450	132,210	116,655	116,225	128,440	139,251	145,373	151,092

[a] Residual contains gross business savings and statistical discrepancy.

ance for Czechoslovakia would be purely arbitrary. Even in the United States, where the national-income accounts are prepared with the greatest of care and where huge amounts of statistical data are available, only 43 per cent of the capital consumption allowance is estimated on the basis of accounting records prepared for income-tax purposes. "The remainder of the allowance is estimated on the basis of a wide variety of sources and methods, and some of them are subject to a wide margin of error."

If in the United States, with its highly developed statistical service, the capital consumption allowance is hardly more than an arbitrary estimate, no more could be done for Czechoslovakia than to take some fixed percentage of the gross product and consider it as representing the capital consumption allowance. Such pretense of precision where it does not exist would be neither desirable nor useful.

Table 12 presents the estimate of the sources and uses of the gross national product in money terms.

PART II

Gross National Product in Real Terms

5

Real Consumption Expenditures

THE CALCULATION of real consumption expenditures is based on the deflation by a price index of the series showing consumption in money terms. For the years 1946 through 1952 I have prepared my own price index; it seems to perform very well and withstands numerous checks of consistency and accuracy. Beginning with 1953, however, this price index fails, primarily because after that date the choices open to the consumer became much more numerous than previously had been the case. Up until 1953 I had little difficulty selecting prices for a particular quality of commodity. But after 1953 an item like "men's suits" contained a range of prices from which it became increasingly difficult and finally impossible to select the price of the suit of "medium quality" that should enter the index. Thus I liquidated my estimate.

COMPOSITION OF AUTHOR'S PRICE INDEX

The basis for my calculation is a revised version of the official "Cost-of-Living Index for a Working-Class Family in Prague." This index was prepared by the State Statistical Office of Czechoslovakia and is based on the Prague Families' Expenditures Study carried out in 1927 and 1928. The composition of the index was originally based on July, 1914, prices. Later the index was recalculated with March, 1939, prices as the base. The index was carried back to June, 1923, and continuous data are available from that time until December, 1949, when the Government of Czechoslovakia ceased to publish any aggregate data on the movements of prices.

In the official index I made several adjustments. Four items were eliminated altogether: income taxes, health-insurance expenditures (which during the period under study were deducted from gross incomes), old-age insurance expenditures (which were consolidated with health insurance and deducted after 1948), and union dues. With respect to union dues, the facts are not clear-cut. In some enterprises they are still collected by union officials; in other enterprises they are deducted directly from wage payments. Many benefits provided by the state depend on the payment of these dues; the labor unions are completely state-dominated and state-subsidized. On this basis I decided that union dues, broadly speaking, should be considered income deductions and treated as such. The items I excluded accounted in 1947 for 14 per cent of expenditures on goods and services included in the index; in 1927, for 1 per cent.

TREATMENT OF FREE-MARKET PRICES

Until January, 1949, the goods included in the official cost-of-living index were either rationed or free, with all goods being sold ostensibly for a single, state-regulated price. In January, 1949, the government introduced the so-called "free market," in which goods identical with goods sold in the rationed market sold at prices considerably higher than the goods on the rationed market. Therefore, I faced two problems. For the period 1945–48, only an official index based on the state-controlled prices was available. To make this index useful, black-market prices had to be integrated with it. And for the period 1949–53, in which dual prices were introduced, no official index was published.

I resolved the difficulty by calculating two indexes. The first is based only on the prices of rationed goods; the second is based on prices of goods traded on the black market during the period 1946–48 and of goods traded on the government free market in the period 1949–53. These two indexes set the limit to the actual change in the level of prices. They are shown in columns 1 and 3 of Table 13.

UNIFIED INDEX FOR TWO SETS OF PRICES

Although these indexes are useful in that they establish the lower and upper limits of price movements during the period under study, they are not really adequate. If the price level of rationed goods in April, 1947, is taken as 100, the index for the rationed market during the year 1952 shows a rise to 198.63, while the index for the free market shows a rise to 493.11. It would be desirable to narrow this broad area of uncertainty and, if possible, arrive at some unique number expressing the price rise during this period.

In 1953 a list of commodities was published in Czechoslovakia stating the total value of sales of these commodities as a fraction of sales on the free market in 1952. Thanks to this piece of evidence, I could calculate the ratios of the quantities of goods sold

TABLE 13

ADJUSTED REVISED COST-OF-LIVING INDEX, 1945–53
(Lower Limit of Revised Cost-of-Living Index for April, 1947 = 100)

Year	Month	Lower Limit: Prices of Rationed Goods	Cost-of-Living Index	Upper Limit: Prices of Unrationed Goods
1945........	May	56.04	n.a.	n.a.
	Nov.	58.48	n.a.	n.a.
	Dec.	70.78	n.a.	n.a.
1946........	Mar.	106.41	132.83	239.58
	June	104.79	124.82	205.20
	Sept.	103.64	116.40	167.15
	Dec.	104.46	115.83	160.63
1947........	Mar.	106.05	115.03	150.79
	June	99.54	111.18	156.95
	Sept.	97.42	113.61	177.21
	Dec.	98.98	120.40	205.48
1948........	Mar.	100.29	128.10	237.53
	June	101.83	138.39	283.21
	Sept.	97.28	142.88	320.67
	Dec.	99.75	153.86	364.22
1949........	....	142.06	186.67	381.79
1950........	....	157.85	194.54	347.54
1951........	....	181.97	215.79	271.19
1952........	....	198.64	252.69	493.11
1953........	June	274.20	274.20	274.20
	Oct.	265.11	265.11	265.11

on the free market to the total quantity sold, and then apply these ratios to the dual prices of goods included in my index.

The next problem was to extend this method for years other than 1952.

For 1949–53 the weights applied to the dual free market and rationed market prices of different commodities in the year 1952 were kept constant over time and used in the calculation of the cost-of-living index. It may be useful, for the sake of clarity, to express the construction of this index symbolically:

$$I_n = \frac{p_{i_n} \, q_{i_{1928}}}{p_{i_{1947}} \, q_{i_{1928}}} \, 100 \, , \tag{1}$$

$$p_{i_n} = \frac{(p_{f_n} \, q_{f_{1952}}) + (p_{r_n} \, q_{r_{1952}})}{q_{f_{1952}} + q_{r_{1952}}} \, . \tag{2}$$

Here I_n stands for the price index in the year n, p_{i_n} for the weighted average price of the ith good in year n, p_{r_n} for the price charged in year n for the good to those consumers who had ration coupons, p_{f_n} for the price charged to those customers who either did not receive or who already used up their ration coupons. The symbol q represents the quantity weights.

The final adjusted revised cost-of-living index for the entire period is presented in column 2 of Table 13. The revised cost-of-living index is repeated here to facilitate comparison.

INDEX FOR THE PERIOD 1954–58

As I pointed out in the introduction to this chapter, my attempt to continue the index after 1953 met with failure. The main reason for this failure was the drastic increase in the range and variety of goods available to the customer after 1953; this increase made it impossible to select on the basis of available data the prices that should enter the index. Depending on the inclination of the researcher, this index could be made to show either a drastic price increase or a drastic price decrease. Neither interpretation could with any degree of honesty be presented to the reader. For that reason I decided to accept the official index covering this period (Table 14).

While my own index, based on the official index covering the period 1930–48, contains less than one hundred commodities, the official index covering the period 1953–58 contains almost five hundred commodities. As Table 14 indicates, these two indexes show quite different changes in the level of prices from 1937 to 1953. The new official index covering the period beginning with the year 1953 shows prices to be 17.9 per cent lower in June, 1953, than my own index based on the old official index shows them to be.

This difference between the two indexes does not necessarily indicate error or bias in either index. As was pointed out, the new official index is based on 1955 patterns of consumer purchases. The old official index, on which my index is based, uses the Laspeyres method: prewar quantities are used to weigh current prices. The new official index essentially represents the Paasche method: 1955 quantities are used to weigh prewar prices. The relative position of the two indexes is the one we would find if

TABLE 14

PRICE INDEX OF CONSUMER GOODS, 1946–58

(1947 = 100)

Year	Official Index I and My Index	Official Index II	Combined Index
1937..................	179.8	100.0	....
1946..................	106.5	....	106.5
1947..................	100.0	....	100.0
1948..................	122.3	....	122.3
1949..................	162.3	....	162.3
1950..................	169.1	....	169.1
1951..................	187.6	....	187.6
1952..................	219.7	....	219.7
1953 (Jan.–May)........	219.7	....	....
1953 (June–Sept.).......	238.7	....	....
1953 (Oct.–Dec.)........	230.5	....	....
1953..................	228.9	134.4	228.9
1954..................	....	129.9	221.3
1955..................	....	126.5	215.4
1956..................	....	123.2	209.8
1957..................	....	120.8	205.7
1958..................	....	120.6	205.4

were we to apply to *identical* price and quantity data Laspeyres' and Paasche's indexes: the prewar basket of consumer goods would be more expensive in 1953 than the postwar basket of consumer goods in 1937. Thus the relation of the two indexes is the one we would expect on the basis of general statistical reasoning.

The final problem is how to link these two indexes. From the official data we know the relation of my extension of the official Index I with the official Index II in June, 1953. But there are no official data for the prereform period (January–May, 1953); and the high degree of confusion existing just before the monetary reform made it impossible for me to prepare price estimates for this period. In some of my previous writings I have made the assumption that in the first half of 1953 prices continued to rise as in the preceding years. Official Index II throws doubt on this assumption: the annual average for 1953 is lower than the level of the index either in June, 1953, or in October, 1953. This suggests that the official index for the first half of the period is lower than the official index for the postreform period. I have calculated th price level for the January–May period implicit in the official Index II and have accepted these data as given and correct.

The combined index shown in Table 14 has been used to deflate personal consumption expeditures and thus to obtain these expenditures in real terms.

6

Other Components of Real Gross National Product

IN THIS CHAPTER I shall discuss the calculation of governmental expenditures in real terms, of investment expenditures in real terms, my inability to convert net foreign investments into real terms, and the conversion of investments into emergency stocks of consumer goods into a monetary unit of constant purchasing power.

GOVERNMENT EXPENDITURES IN REAL TERMS

The deflating index for government expenditures on goods and services is a composite index that uses the prices of investment

TABLE 15

PRICE INDEX OF GOVERNMENT-PURCHASED
SERVICES, 1946–58
(1948 = 100)

Year	Index	Year	Index
1946	79.5	1953	145.0
1947	92.8	1954	155.9
1948	100.0	1955	159.5
1949	105.2	1956	165.7
1950	117.5	1957	169.0
1951	129.1	1958	172.5
1952	139.8		

goods and the changes in wages and salaries. On the basis of the budgets for the years 1946–49, I calculated that on the average 60 per cent of the expenditures went to state employees and 40 per cent went to purchase goods from other sectors of the economy. The price index for personal services is again a combined index of the wages paid to manual workers and salaries paid to other employees. On the basis of the budget for the year 1946, I calculated the ratio of manual workers to white-collar workers in government employment. Roughly 75 per cent of government employees were salaried employees, and 25 per cent were workers receiving weekly or semimonthly wages. These weights, applied

41

to the index of wages and salaries, yielded the values stated in Table 15.

NET FOREIGN INVESTMENT IN REAL TERMS

This part of the gross national product I was unable to deflate, because no detailed figures exist that could be used for the task. Because this segment constitutes such a minute part of the gross national product, the error caused by the failure to deflate may be considered very small.

GROSS DOMESTIC INVESTMENT IN REAL TERMS

In the case of gross domestic investment, the most promising approach was not to look for a price index that could be used to deflate money values but to discover the real value of investment in each year. Only afterward were implicit deflators calculated for comparison with other price indexes.

For the period 1947–53 the investment both in money and in real terms is known. As far as the real terms are concerned, they are expressed in prices of different origin, but in each case one can discern the shift from the monetary unit of one purchasing power to the monetary unit of another purchasing power. The 1948 prices were 22.2 per cent higher than the 1947 prices; the 1948 prices, in terms of which the first two years of the Plan were measured, were raised by 29.3 per cent when the planners shifted their accounts to a higher price level more suitable for the preparation of the revisions introduced during the last three years of the Five-Year Plan. The resulting estimates are shown in Table 16.

Official indexes published subsequently conflict in several respects with my own estimates (Table 17). It will be noticed that all estimates of the level of real investments for the year 1950 are exceedingly close to each other. The year 1949 shows a discrepancy; the official indexes are much higher than my own index. Because my index is based on contemporary data published by the government, I have more confidence in it than in the official data published seven years afterward. The next discrepancy comes with respect to the year 1951. My index shows no change; the official index shows an increase by 20 to 21 per cent. In view of the fact that the State Statistical Office announced in the 1952 report on plan-fulfilment that the level of investments in 1951 remained the same as in 1950, the official claim made for this year seven years later seems less than credible. The difference between my estimate and the official estimate for the year 1952 is negligible; so these estimates agree. The next discrepancy comes in the case of 1953. My figures show a slight decrease; official

TABLE 16

REAL INVESTMENTS, 1946–58

Year	Real Investments (Millions of Crowns[a])	Base Year for Prices	Real Investments (Base Year = 1947)
1946.........	3,250	1946	3,533
1947.........	4,950	1947	4,950
1948.........	7,160	1947	7,158
1949.........	10,116	1948	8,283
1950.........	14,162	1948	11,589
1951.........	18,310	1950	11,591
1952.........	20,637	1950	13,065
1953.........	19,827	1950	12,551
1953.........	(19,784)	(1959)	(12,551)
1954.........	19,198	1959	12,180
1955.........	19,931	1959	12,644
1956.........	24,544	1959	15,635
1957.........	26,806	1959	17,005
1958.........	30,423	1959	19,300

[a] Purchasing power as of base year (col. 2).

TABLE 17

COMPARISON OF VARIOUS ESTIMATES OF REAL INVESTMENTS, 1948–53

Year	My Index	Official Index I (1956 Prices)	Official Index II (1957 Prices)	Official Index III (1959 Prices)	Annual Percentage Changes in My Index	Annual Percentage Changes in Index I	Annual Percentage Changes in Index II	Annual Percentage Changes in Index III
1948...	100	100	100	100	....	....	....	....
1949...	116	132	132	132	16	32	32	32
1950...	162	159	159	159	39	20	20	20
1951...	162	192	192	192	0	21	21	20
1952...	183	225	225	225	13	17	17	17
1953...	175	229	229	231	− 4	2	2	3

TABLE 18

INDEX OF PRICES OF GROSS NATIONAL PRODUCT

Type of Disbursement	1946	1947	1948	1949	1950	1951	1952	1953	1954	1955	1956	1957	1958
Consumer purchases	87.1	81.7	100.0	132.7	138.3	153.4	179.6	186.9	180.6	176.0	171.3	168.0	167.7
Gross domestic investment	75.3	81.8	100.0	176.0	173.3	208.0	197.7	150.7	128.4	145.4	143.2	144.5	128.6
Government purchases:													
Of goods	75.3	81.8	100.0	176.0	173.3	208.0	197.7	150.7	128.4	145.4	143.2	144.5	128.6
Of services	79.5	92.8	100.0	105.2	117.5	129.1	139.8	145.0	155.9	159.5	165.7	169.0	172.5
Government purchases of emergency stocks	.....	.....	100.0	.....	.....	153.4	179.6	186.9	.....	.....	.....	.....	.....
Net foreign investment	75.3	81.8	100.0	176.0	173.3	208.0	197.7	150.7	128.4	145.4	143.2	144.5	128.6
Gross national product	83.9	83.1	100.0	140.3	145.9	161.5	176.9	184.6	160.5	164.9	161.4	160.6	154.3

TABLE 19

GROSS NATIONAL PRODUCT IN CONSTANT CROWNS, 1946–58

(In Millions of 1948 Crowns)

Type of Disbursement	1946	1947	1948	1949	1950	1951	1952	1953	1954	1955	1956	1957	1958
Consumer purchases	29,601	37,269	36,513	33,143	39,262	40,007	39,098	34,410	39,292	43,136	47,445	51,538	51,593
Gross domestic investment	4,317	6,048	8,746	10,120	14,160	14,162	15,963	15,335	14,881	15,449	19,103	20,777	23,580
Government investments (+) or disinvestments (−) in emergency stocks	0	0	0	0	+ 0	+ 214	+ 2,193	− 2,407	0	0	0	0	0
Net foreign investment	− 2,285	− 1,759	860	103	511	591	15	788	406	610	1,013	144	873
Government purchases of goods and services	12,182	11,438	10,944	7,678	9,410	12,170	17,459	15,051	17,841	18,671	18,699	18,305	21,825
Real gross national product	43,815	52,996	55,343	51,044	63,343	67,144	74,728	63,177	72,420	77,866	86,260	90,476	97,871
Index	79.2	95.7	100.0	92.2	114.4	121.3	135.0	114.1	130.8	140.7	151.9	163.5	176.8

figures of 1957 show a slight increase. Yet, only half a year earlier *Rudé Právo* reported (June 20, 1956), "in the years 1953 through 1955 we failed to reach the level of investments reached in the year 1952." Thus even with respect to 1953, the contemporary data, supported by the statement above, seem more trustworthy than the claims made in 1957 and subsequent years.

GROSS NATIONAL PRODUCT IN REAL TERMS

It now becomes possible to deflate all the components of the gross national product. The price deflators used are presented in Table 18, while the gross national product expressed in terms of a monetary unit of constant purchasing power appears in Table 19.

7

Conclusion: Inputs versus Useful Outputs

WE HAVE COME to the end of the road with the national-income accounts lying in front of us. I entrust my figures to others with some trepidation for, as Professor Milton Friedman once said, statistics are like children: after they are released from parental custody they acquire a life of their own, independent of their maker. Accordingly, I want to devote this chapter to a last-minute attempt to assure that the life my figures lead will be a responsible one.[1]

In general, there is only a very imperfect nexus between national-income data and an index of the welfare of the nation. Some limitations of national-income accounts in this respect are extremely well understood. For instance, the fact is well realized, even though frequently neglected, that income accounts measure only items that pass through the market and a few imputed items. They do not measure any sizable portion of output that does not pass through the market. A prime example of this case is the services of women. Whenever a housewife enters the labor force, national income increases by the full amount of her output, and no subtraction is made of the output lost to the household sector. Special problems, however, face the user of national-income accounts prepared for a country that organizes its production according to principles different from those existing in countries for which the national-income accounting methods have originally been worked out. Specifically, grave problems appear when we follow the standard interpretation of national-income accounts in the case of centrally directed economies in general and of the Soviet-bloc countries in particular. The rules that any society must follow to achieve maximum output are well known; the body of price theory, restated in the Lerner-Lange model for a socialistic society, expresses these rules. But the consequences of ignoring these rules in our interpretation of national-income accounts have not been adequately discussed.

[1] I am greatly indebted to Abba P. Lerner, who contributed many valuable suggestions when I was writing this chapter.

INCOME ACCOUNTING: SOME ASSUMPTIONS

The National Income Division of the Department of Commerce states that "the first task of national-income accounting is to delimit economic production from the pursuit of other activities that resemble it in that they involve the use of human effort and other resources and are useful."[2] The key word in this sentence is the word "useful." Goods that qualify for entry into the accounts are entered by the amount of their usefulness, measured by price.

The justification for this index of usefulness is obvious. Regardless of the amount of resources used up in the production of any particular good, this good, before being entered into the national-income account, must find a purchaser who, by sacrificing an amount of his resources equal to the price, certifies that the usefulness of the good is equal to this price. If the price is equal to the value of resources used up, then this good enters the product side of the accounts at this value; and there is a corresponding entry on the income side of the accounts in the form of wages, salaries, rents, profits, etc. Suppose, however, that an incompetent producer uses up a greater amount of resources than necessary in producing the good. In such a case he will find a purchaser only if he sells the good at a price lower than the cost of resources he has used up. The good will enter the product side of the accounts by a measure of usefulness that is smaller than the costs; on the income side of the accounts the payments made by the producer to his factors of production appear as before. His own income, however, will be shown to be zero or negative, and thus the two sides again balance. Obviously, if all the purchasers were willing (as, for instance, the government at times is willing) to purchase a good on a "cost-plus" basis, the national-income accounts would show simply the resources used up in the productive process, not useful output produced. Normally, however, purchasers are not that generous. Thus the meaning of the national-income accounts crucially depends on the reliability of the judges who certify to the usefulness of any good purchased. How reliable are these judges?

[2] U.S.D.C., *National Income, 1954*, p. 30.

Two problems arise in answering this question. One problem is the diligence of the judges; another is whether the economic organization makes the task of judges of given diligence easy or difficult. I shall take up these two related but distinct issues in turn.

DILIGENCE IN EVALUATING USEFUL OUTPUT

Economists start with the assumption that the tastes of the consumers are given and that, given such tastes and the income constraint, the consumers attempt to maximize satisfaction. Thus, whenever a consumer has to back up his decision on the usefulness of a good by sacrificing his own resources, we are bound to conclude that this consumer is a most diligent judge of the usefulness of the goods he buys. In the case of an investor who uses his own funds, the same reasoning holds. Doubt is bound to appear in the case of an investor who uses "someone else's money." Here the necessity of exercising diligence as a judge of usefulness is less direct and is closely related to the second aspect of the question, the problem of economic organization. For instance, the smaller the socially permissible competition among managers, the smaller will be the average efficiency of these managers in judging the usefulness of goods.

In the case of government purchases of goods and services, the problem becomes extremely difficult indeed. First, "someone else's money" is always used, and the rewards of the decision-maker are completely unrelated to his ability to obtain maximum usefulness for the dollars he spends. Second, even if the purchaser holds elective office, the majority that elects him may not be the majority that pays the taxes. And if his office is not elective, we cannot assume that his decisions on usefulness follow the desires of those who pay the bill to any degree at all. All this suggests that the government is bound to judge the usefulness of many goods it buys in a way that would not be followed by the tax-payers themselves. Third, the task of the government itself is so immensely complex that no simple criterion (such as profit in the case of businesses) is applicable. Thus the decision-maker is bound to be a less efficient judge of the usefulness of goods than is a private individual.

This would end our essentially negative evaluation of the economic performance of the government if it were not for one essential fact. Experience shows that our assumption that consumers always know what is best for them and act accordingly is itself not correct: since the beginning of time the government has interfered with private decisions and has frequently found overwhelming support for such interference. This suggests that the consumers also like to purchase the services of government officials whose sole task is to coerce them into doing what they feel they should do but would not do of their own volition. This, of course, means that the consumers admit that the government, in some instances, is a better judge of the usefulness of goods than they are.

Because of all these difficulties it might perhaps be best to separate the private and government output and to refuse to show the sum; the summation is bound to contain items that are qualitatively so different as not to be additive. This radical suggestion, however, is not likely to meet with much favor. Obviously, in my accounts I have followed the conventional definition of the gross national product.

FACILITIES FOR THE EVALUATION OF THE
USEFULNESS OF GOODS

The second problem concerns the type of economic organization in which those who judge the usefulness of any good operate. Even a purchaser of consumption goods who is the most diligent of judges may operate extremely inefficiently in certain situations. In the classical case of a natural monopoly he will attach a positive price to output whose resource cost is zero simply because the economic organization in which he operates permits this monopoly. In general we may say that the consumer is able to downgrade the usefulness of goods satisfactory to him to the resource cost and to downgrade the usefulness of goods not satisfactory to him below the resource cost only if he is free to purchase the goods from competitive suppliers. Thus by now it is unnecessary to point out that competition and national-income accounts are most intimately related: without competition, goods will enter national-income accounts at a value higher than they would otherwise.

In the absence of diligence on the side of the purchasers, goods would enter the accounts at purely hapazard values. In the presence of diligence but in the absence of competition, two possibilities appear. If a good already in existence becomes subject to monopolistic practices, whether in the sense that the producer is able to reap excess profits or in the sense that his position enables him to use resources wastefully, the price index used to deflate money values will assure that the good will continue to be entered in the national-income accounts expressed in real terms according to its original index of usefulness, the premonopoly price. In the case of all new goods, however, this corrective function of the price index fails us. The good will be entered by its full price, which contains also a return to the seller who contributes nothing to production but the ability to monopolize. In such cases the income accounts will fail to measure growth in the total useful output; instead, they will measure a quantity exceeding this amount by the rewards paid to the monopolist if he is a profit maximizer or to other factors of production if he chooses to dissipate monopolistic returns by an excessive use of such factors.

CRITERIA DETERMINING THE USEFULNESS
CONTENT OF INCOME

It is now apparent that our interpretation of the national-income accounts depends crucially on the satisfaction of the maximizing conditions specified by economic theory. Of special importance, when we discuss the accounts prepared for any country of the Soviet bloc, are these two restrictions: purchasers have to be adequately motivated to evaluate diligently the usefulness of goods, and they must face sellers who are either competitive or, as in the Lange-Lerner model, forced to operate as if they were competitive. The more closely these conditions are satisfied, the more closely will the national-income accounts measure the *useful* output produced; the less they are satisfied, the more nearly will these accounts measure simply the cost of the resources used up in the productive process.

No country will fully satisfy the maximization conditions, and no country will completely fail to satisfy them; any differences we find will be differences of degree. Since income accounts do not exist that measure the performance of an economy perfectly satisfying these criteria, the reader can better judge the income accounts for a country with which he is familiar than the accounts of a strange country. In what follows I attempt to give the reader, very briefly, some explanations that will enable him to understand the meaning of my accounts.

CHARACTER OF THE CZECH ECONOMY

At the outset, a few generalities. In Czechoslovakia, the government purchases almost half the annual output either directly or through its agents, the nationalized industries. With some exceptions in the farm sector, all enterprises are non-competitive: the vast majority of goods is produced by industrial combines that are the sole producers of these particular goods. We may view these combines as monopolistic in nature; or we may view the different plants assembled in a combine as a cartel that is completely protected against invasion by competitors. We cannot, however, put much trust in any description of legal organization. Despite such organization, the producer could still be following the Lange-Lerner rules. Thus it is the behavior of these enterprises that interests us. It should be pointed out that excess monopolistic profits are only one manifestation of monopoly power, a manifestation we are likely to find if the monopolist is a profit maximizer or is permitted to be a profit maximizer. Another manifestation of monopolistic behavior may be a dissipation of the potential profits by excessive use of resources or by the use of inefficient methods of production; indeed, it is precisely this manifestation that we are likely to find in the case of publicly regulated monopolies in the capitalist economy and in the state-operated monopolies in the Soviet type of economy. In what follows I discuss some of the evidence bearing on this topic.

INVESTMENT GOODS

The method of financing investment goods changed frequently during the period covered by my study. During the entire period, however, most investment expenditures were made by the allocation of government funds to enterprises for projects approved by the government. In some cases, the purchases were made from other enterprises that were the sole suppliers of the good in question (e.g., all construction in Czechoslovakia is undertaken by one construction combine); in other cases, the purchasing enterprise bought goods from itself.

There is substantial evidence that many of the goods produced would not have passed the market test. By that I mean that the investment goods would not have been purchased if the purchaser had used his own funds rather than government allocations or if the buyer could have turned to an alternative source of supply. A few items may be mentioned simply to illustrate the magnitude of the problem.

Until 1952 all business and industrial construction was entrusted to one architectural combine. The economic performance of this combine, and thus the salaries and premiums paid to its managers and employees, was measured by the gross value of the projects undertaken by the combine. It was discovered that the system of incentives worked as any economist would predict: plants and office buildings were planned to be as ornate as possible, the materials specified in the plans were consistently of the highest quality, floor and walls were designed to have strength much in excess of the expected load factors. The more expensive a building, the more it contributed to the measured output of this architectural combine. Clearly, the resources used up during this period substantially exceeded the useful output produced.

In the early fifties the construction industry adopted a new technique of construction based on the assembly of prefabricated sections of outside and inside walls. Early in 1964 a group of construction engineers complained that all efforts to induce the industry to shift to a cheaper method of pouring concrete between prefabricated, reusable forms failed because the new method would idle most of the equipment necessary for the production, transportation, and assembly of the prefabricated wall sections. Since the construction industry receives premiums based on an index showing the degree of utilization of the capital equipment it owns, the new method would result in lowering incomes in the construction industry.

Again, in the early sixties there appeared a report that some ten years previously a group of engineers had invented a new loom that utilized pneumatic rather than mechanical transmission of power and was allegedly much more efficient. As a proof of efficiency it was mentioned that the Swiss subsequently invented an identical machine and experienced an excellent selling record. The Czech machine industry refused to accept the innovation because to do so would have required retooling of several plants; during retooling the plants could not fulfil their planned output and consequently would lose the premiums paid for such fulfilment.

Finally, the economic journals contain constant complaints that people who are called "regional patriots" attempt to obtain additional factories by deliberately understating the cost of planned investment projects. Apparently the safest way of doing so is to cost correctly only the main project and not to specify ancillary investment at all. In one case, which has been discussed at some length as one of the worst cases on record, a plant was built that could become operational only after construction of a bridge to tie the plant to the railroad net and after construction of a dam to supply necessary water. Provided that in this case the planners did not seriously underestimate the contribution of the new plant to output, resources used up must have exceeded useful output produced.

CONSUMPTION

In the case of consumption goods, the Czechoslovak consumer is no doubt as diligent in evaluating useful output as the consumer of any other country. But he is faced by producers who are not competitive. The question then arises: Do the producers in Czechoslovakia behave like monopolies? They have to sell the plan-determined value of output and thus they *are* competing for the consumer's dollar. But there is only one combine producing a given good and this combine is therefore not competitive so far as the goods it produces are concerned. The choice the consumer has in such a case is very limited: he is free either to buy or go without a given commodity.

Thus, obviously, the possibility of exploiting the consumer depends on the elasticity of his demand for any given commodity.

Prices at which the enterprises must sell are fixed by the state, normally so as to express the average cost of production of all the plants producing a given item: the enterprises are not free to determine an optimum price as a textbook monopolist is. But they do seem to be able to change the nature of the product itself, decrease the average and marginal cost, and achieve a higher than competitive price in this roundabout way.

For instance, the planners found it convenient to plan the output of numerous enterprises in terms of weight: so many tons of pots and pans, so many tons of furniture, so many tons of lighting fixtures. Control over the economic performance of the enterprises is exerted mainly through control of the wage bill. Finally, the planners attempt to assure that useful output will be produced by requiring the enterprises to fulfil a sales plan. It did not take the enterprises long to discover that the use of excessive amounts of raw materials would enable them to fulfil and overfulfil all three of these criteria and thus earn the crucial premium. In the first place, an inconveniently heavy article, say a lighting fixture, will be sold anyway because the demand for the article is more inelastic than it would be if other suppliers were free to produce a more desirable good. Thus the sales plan is fulfilled. In the second place, the heavier the fixture, the bigger its contribution to the planned tonnage of output. The burden of fulfilling the plan is thus shifted to the producers of raw materials. Finally, the cost of machining and assembly is unrelated to the weight of the article: the heavier the unit, the smaller the labor content per unit of output and the easier it is to fulfil the planned wage bill.

Thus, as the Czech press complains, the small apartments now being built are crammed with over-sized furniture and are lit by fixtures that, as one official remarked in a humorous vein, require a steel beam imbedded in the ceiling to hold them up. Obviously, the resources used up in the production of these goods exceed substantially the value of useful output.

There are many complaints on the extremely shabby quality of consumer goods and on the big percentage of export items that are either returned or on which price concessions have to be made. The temptation to recount some of the cases here is great, but it must be resisted because by the very nature of consumption goods any item that could be mentioned (razor blades, toothbrushes, pens, pencils, etc.) is relatively inconsequential. Only a huge mass of examples would impart to the reader an idea of the magnitude of the problem. One reason for the poor quality of goods is that the quality-controllers in the enterprise must "live with" their fellow workers. Plant committees decide who gets and who does not get an apartment; their reports seriously affect whether the children of the employees will be permitted to enter the senior high school and the university, etc. Under these conditions an energetic controller who would refuse to accept goods and thus affect the ability of the enterprise to fulfil the plan is in a very weak position. The purchasing agents for the retail trade frequently depend on the co-operation of the enterprise: if they are stubborn in the case of one item, they may find it difficult to purchase another item. Even if they do object, the plants apparently have a tendency to send delegations of employees to plead with the agents. The delegations argue that the raw materials they had to use were poor, that the machinery they have is obsolete, and that refusal of the output will thus unjustly penalize the plant. Whatever the marketing process is, the fact remains that the consumers are paying a price set for a given product of given quality but are receiving an inferior substitute. This is the same as if they were paying a higher price for the given product.

WEALTH

Finally, there is a shortcoming in the national-income accounting method that results in registering what is actually a negative output as a positive output. The national-income accountants found it impossible to measure the income yielded by most of the real wealth owned by the final consumer. The sole exception was the value of income yielded by private houses; this frequently appears as an imputed item. Suppose that a refrigerator-producer, facing an increased demand for spare parts, is planning to increase the output of spare parts during the current income period. Suppose further that he is ordered to use his resources to produce an additional number of finished refrigerators. From the standpoint of national-income accounts, this change in the structure of output will be of no consequence. Regardless of whether the output is increased by a given quantity of spare parts or by a quantity of refrigerators of equal value, either increase will be registered as the same increase in output. But the real result of the increased output of finished refrigerators is a decrease in the true national income: the addition of a given number of new refrigerators increases the stock of wealth by the value of these new refrigerators, while the resulting lack of spare parts decreases the stock of wealth by some multiple of this value. The decrease is a multiple of the value because each new refrigerator contains parts that could keep many older refrigerators operational. The consequence of the hypothetical order given to the refrigerator-producer is an increase in registered national income accompanied by a decrease in the true income yielded by wealth. This shortcoming of the national-income accounting method is of small consequence in a market-directed economy: there a demand for spare parts automatically brings forth a supply of spare parts. Given the notorious shortages of spare parts registered in all countries of the Soviet bloc, however, the problem just raised is extremely important for our interpretation of national-income accounts prepared for these countries.

As usual, the reasons for the lack of spare parts in Czechoslovakia are complex. One cause is to be found in the method by which production is organized: frequently the output of finished goods is planned in terms of numbers and the output of parts in terms of tons. This has the consequences already discussed. Second, it appears that the prices of spare parts are set at levels that make output of finished goods more attractive to the enterprises. Third, the lack of spare parts at times is used by monopolist producers as another tool for exploiting the consumer. Lack of a part might force the consumer to purchase a new commodity and thus increase the sales of a given enterprise. For instance, some time ago there was a notorious case involving vacuum bottles with plastic tops that broke easily and were irreplaceable. A diligent reporter traced the causes and discovered that the enterprise producing the bottles signed a contract with the producer of plastic tops that bound the plastics manufacturer to produce only the number of caps needed for newly produced bottles. When one and the same enterprise is producing both the finished goods and the parts, the problem of discovery and proof becomes extremely difficult: every breakdown of machinery, every failure of the suppliers of raw materials is used to explain the low output of spare parts. At the end of the year the guilty enterprise is bound to have an extensive list of "objective difficulties"—which excuse non-performance of the plan—as a result of which sufficient quantities of spare parts could not be produced.

The consequences of the lack of spare parts are extremely serious. While increases in consumer durables are registered every year, a part of durables produced in the preceding years is out of operation because some part, often quite trivial, is missing. Industrial machinery and farm machinery are frequently out of order for the same reason. In the case of productive facilities, inoperative machinery shows as a negative item in the national-income account by leading to a lower output than would have been obtained otherwise; consequently it often forces even plants that otherwise would not utilize their monopoly power over the consumer to use it and thus to recover losses. At the same time, enterprises use expensive machinery to supply themselves with parts that, if mass-produced, could be obtained at a fraction of the resources used up. Finally, shortages and erratic supply of spare parts force enterprises to maintain excessive inventories.

In this chapter I have stated certain elementary economic propositions concerning the maximization of output and have related these propositions to the national-income accounts and the meaning of these accounts. It seemed advisable to me to do this because many of us suffer from a certain compartmentation of thought: in our models we use the established body of economic theory, but in our empirical work we tend to use national-income accounts for the most dissimilar countries as if these accounts were interchangeable. Once standard economic theory is related to national-income accounts, it becomes obvious that these accounts, superficially so objective, are actually closely tied to the economic organization of the particular state for which they are prepared. For this reason, therefore, I have argued that it is desirable to view the income accounts prepared for a country like Czechoslovakia—which does not organize production by permitting and enforcing competitive processes—simply as a measure of the resources the country can mobilize to produce goods and services, not as a measure of useful output.

Index

59